TRAVELING CARAVAN

Growing up under the Big Top

WRITTEN BY
KRISTIN L. SCHMIDT LARSON

DEDICATION

I dedicate this book to my father, Harold Stephan Schmidt.

Thank you to my Aunt Darlene Schmidt Fortune for all her contributions to the book.
Thank you to my departed grandmother, Phyllis, who taught me never to give up and always be kind to everyone.
Thank you to my departed grandfather, Harold E. Schmidt, who had a vision to entertain thousands of people and brought laughter and joy to people's lives with the Schmidt Family Circus.
To my entire Schmidt family, this book is a part of all of you. I love you all.

AUTHOR'S PREFACE

My grandfather, Harold Earl Schmidt, traveled with his One-Man Band in the 1930s and 1940s. He married my grandmother Phyllis Maas, and they had four children, including my father, the eldest, Harold Stephan Schmidt. All the children grew up Under the Big Top. The Circus became a traveling carnival in the late 1960s as the children graduated from college. I traveled the Midwest during my teenage years with my family's carnival. It was arduous work, and the experiences opened my eyes to the fact that we were treated differently and referred to as Carni people. I knew at a youthful age what it felt like to be excluded and treated second class. Our days were long, and the carnival business was lucrative and risky due to the liability of the carnival rides. This book is non-fiction, featuring my family members and towns along the way.

Keep the circus going inside you,
keep it going, don't take anything too
seriously, it'll all work out in the end.

David Niven

THE HAPPY MERRY-GO-ROUND

Happy music from the Merry-Go-Round was heard throughout the carnival.

Children dash to reach the Merry-Go-Round. Their parents follow closely behind.

The bright, shiny colored lights remind them of Christmas.

The colorful, magical horses move up and down like moments in our lives.

The children laugh joyfully, bringing smiles to their parents' faces.

The merry-go-round moves round and round until it slowly moves to a complete stop.

The happy music continues to play as the children disappear down the carnival midway.

Written by Kristin Schmidt Larson

SCHMIDT'S

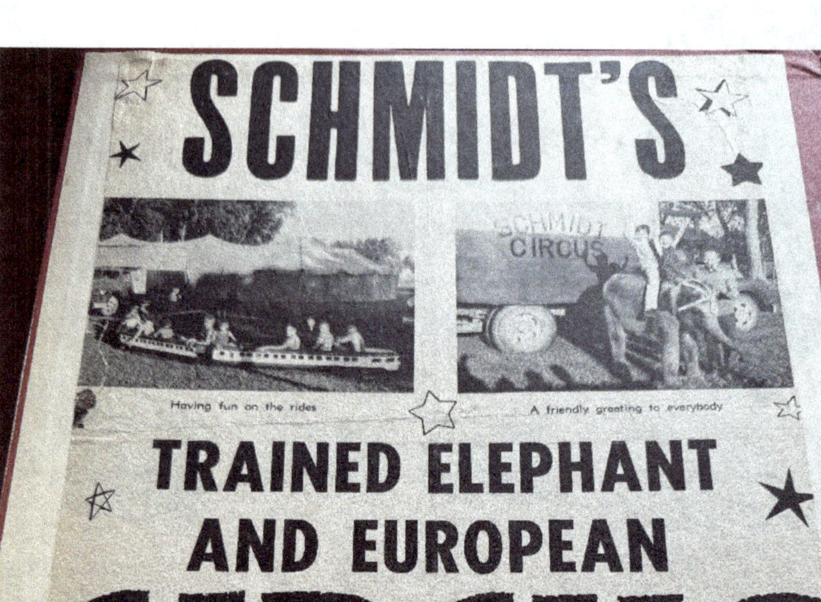

Having fun on the rides

A friendly greeting to everybody

TRAINED ELEPHANT
AND EUROPEAN
CIRCUS

**FREE   FREE
CIRCUS
COUPONS
INSIDE**

Our Motto:

"GOOD CLEAN ENTERTAINMENT"

Clergymen Invited

CIRCUS PRICES

PRE-SALE: 40c - 80c

GATE SALE: 50c and $1.00

Rides 8 for $1.00, pre-sale,
or 25c on grounds.

TABLE OF CONTENT

CHAPTER 1:

SCHMIDT FAMILY CIRCUS: WORLD'S LARGEST ONE-MAN-BAND

My grandfather, Harold Earl Schmidt (December 6, 1909 - March 5, 1991), was brilliant, creative, and a visionary. He learned to play thirty-two instruments for his One-Man Band. He was a musical genius. He traveled throughout South Dakota and North Dakota during the 1930s and 1940s. He had the largest One-Man Band in the World, documented in **Robert Ripley's Believe It or Not Book**. Harold Schmidt played six instruments simultaneously without electrical power: piano, accordion, guitar, bass fiddle, drums, soc cymbal, and horn. He could play five instruments blindfolded. Harold was also part of the Chuck Olinger Wonder Show, which traveled throughout South Dakota.

There was a playing event near Killdeer, North Dakota, and my grandfather, Harold E Schmidt, met my great-grandmother, Rose Maas. Rose noticed his ability to play several instruments and thought he would be a good provider for her daughter, Phyllis Maas. Rose Maas and Harold E Schmidt arranged the marriage, and Rose received a monetary payment from my grandfather. My grandma was so young, just a child of 16 years old, but Rose had seventeen children to care for, and she was happy and knew that Harold would take loving care of her. Harold and Phyllis drove to Glendive, Montana, and were married in 1942. My grandmother told me she did not have a lovely dress to wear on her wedding day. My grandfather went to the most expensive store in Glendive and bought her a long, delicate blue dress with white flowers. She had never worn anything so beautiful. On January 29, 1943, my father, Harold Stephen. Schmidt was born. They had three more children. Darlene, Boni, and Edward. Some of the children were accomplished musicians who performed acts that became part of the "Schmidt Family Circus," based in Watertown, South Dakota, and they all grew up under the "Big Top."

This type of life was unusual, and the family spoke a carny language. My father also talks about his feelings of exclusion and discrimination.   All the children in the family experienced throughout their childhood and teenage years as they traveled and worked hard. My father would leave school early for the year at the beginning of May and would not be back in school until late September. Therefore, they had to study, be prepared to make up work for school and work on their musical talents.

Boni

Ed

My father tells me stories from his Circus days. One of the first stories my father shared with me was when he asked his dad if he could have an elephant when he was about seven. He told his dad he thought it would be a great animal in their Circus. They already had two monkeys, Oscar and Poncho, Tommy the Lion, Sally the Bear, Silver the Racoon, Snakes, and a gator. and other small animals. My great-aunt Elsie was in attendance during the show. Poncho came down from the stage and pulled her skirt off. Everyone in the audience laughed and. thought it was part of an act. It was not, and she was mortified.

A few years passed, and my father came home from school to see a trailer in the front yard. He could hear a squealing noise coming out from the trailer. He thought it sounded like a pig. But suddenly, he saw a gray trunk sticking out the trailer's back part. His dad told him, *"Look what just arrived for you."* My grandfather opened the back end of the trailer and said to my dad, *'Here is your elephant."* The family named her Rosalita. She had traveled from Mumbai (Bombay), India, to Watertown, South Dakota. The cost of this elephant has never been shared with the family. However, in 1953, it would be a considerable sum of money.

My grandfather made a big trailer for Rosalita to travel between the towns. On the bottom of the trailer, he had an opening that he made so that when the elephant pooped, it would go down into the bottom of a tray. The tray would be open, and farmers would buy this for fertilizer. Rosalita became my father's best friend. He trained her, cared for her, and loved her so much. When Rosalita died, her remains were given to the Natural Science Museum in St. Paul, Minnesota.

A big tent needed to be set up in every town. My father would have to put up the poles and pound in the stakes. Darlene, his sister, would also help with this. It was demanding work. Benches had to be set up. The stage was also set up, with lights hanging from the top of the tent and lights on the bottom of the stage. Three hundred people could watch the show under the Big Top.

My father was a young clown named Doodie. This was his first act in the Circus. At the age of five, my father started learning the accordion. He became an accomplished accordion player and would play music during the Circus acts. Darlene would twirl rings of fire on batons. She could do different acrobats and tap dance. Boni rode the unicycle and juggled. Edward, being the youngest `played the saxophone. My grandmother knew how to use bull whips and ropes. She would have Byron put a cigarette in his mouth and use her bullwhip to whip the end of the cigarette off. My grandfather would have an act with Tojo, the Wonder Dog. Indeed, the animals were the center of the circus. Everyone loved Rosalita.

Leta, the next elephant to join the Circus, was purchased from the Watertown, South Dakota Zoo, and Tanya, another elephant, came from the Como Zoo in St. Paul, Minnesota.

CHAPTER 2:
CARNIVAL CARAVAN: MY GRANDFATHER'S TENT

Phyllis(left) grandmother,
Harold S. Schmidt, father,
Boni, aunt
Byron Osander, step-grandfather on accordion
Edward, uncle
Darlene, aunt

My family-owned and operated MINN-NO-SO-DAK Shows. Our traveling carnival came to a small town in Eureka, South Dakota. I was 11 years old and spent a week with my Aunt Darlene, helping with the carnival. After I went to bed each night, Aunt Darlene firmly instructed me not to leave the trailer and to keep it locked. As the carnival closed for the evening, she went to bed. Later that night, I could hear noises outside the trailer. I peeked out the window and could see three large men taking my grandfather's tent that he used for his games. I quickly awakened my aunt and told her people were taking Grandpa's tent. She quickly put on her clothes, ran out the trailer door barefoot, and ran after the three men who dropped the tent. The following day, I looked at the parking lot she had run across, filled with debris and cracked open glass bottles. It was amazing that her feet did not get hurt. My aunt would do anything to protect my grandfather as he was a person who was ill with Parkinson's disease, diagnosed at the age of thirty, yet still wanted to have a part in the carnival. One of his games was five wooden bowling pins and a softball to throw to get them all down. He had it set up so the children would win a small trinket. He loved to see the smiles on their faces when they won. Another game was throwing the ring on the bottles of pop. He always had his dog, Tojo, right next to him to protect him, and of course, this little dog was his best friend. Tojo could roll on a barrel and dance on his back two legs.

Wherever my grandfather went, Tojo went. We would always help Grandfather disconnect his water hose and electrical cords. When we were ready to leave, Tojo would jump in the old car and sit on the front seat driver's side, waiting for him. We would take off shortly behind him. The traveling carnival caravan would be our old truck with the trailer and the old truck with the concession stand. We would always follow behind Grandfather to ensure he reached the destination, and then the rides would follow one ride after another. The traveling carnival started with only a few rides, such as the jungle gym, the Ferris wheel, the Merry-Go-Round, and other rides added over the years. I reflect on the fact that my grandfather started with his vision of his one-man band, which developed into a family circus with all the children and became a traveling carnival.

In 1965, the carnival relocated to Dalton, Minnesota. My grandparents had divorced, and my grandmother remarried Byron Osander, who was from this area of Minnesota. The winter months were spent in the woods of Dalton, Minnesota, and it was a bit like heaven. They worked on the carnival games and the rides, which needed repair or paint. Also, when booking the summer events, Grandmother would talk to County Fair people and book for the following summer. We would attend carnival trade show events, where county fair people would come and contract for the summer. I attended two of these in Minneapolis, Minnesota.

The place in the country just outside of Dalton was picturesque. There was a small lake nearby. It had a round, red historic barn, where the two elephants, Lita and Tanya, and the mini ponies stayed in the winter months. The rides were kept in a large building, and there was another sizeable, heated building where the repair work was done. A few of the workers stayed on all year long. Dave, who was with the carnival the entire time and lived in the building, had a loft above and Speedy (Nick's name). I never knew his real name.

I was always playing tricks on Dave. One night, I went to his room in the big shop building where his loft was and poured some perfume on his pillow. Another night, I put Vaseline on his doorknob. He would come into the farmhouse in the morning and yell my name up the stairs. He would then laugh, and I ran down the stairs to hug him. He never got mad at me. Dave was just like part of our family. He was like another uncle.

Winnie stayed with our family from the late 1970s until the carnival dissolved in 2007. Winnie was short in stature and had a loud voice. She and Grandmother were similar in that manner. She knew how to work just like the men and sometimes even harder. She was always with the family for every holiday and lived in a bedroom on the farmhouse in the winter months. She was also like family, like another aunt. These were some of the best days of my childhood: traveling to small towns, learning about people with the carnival caravan, and spending time with my family.

At Christmastime, my family would pack up the station wagon and head north to Grandma's house on Dalton Mountain. As young kids, we thought it looked like a mountain, but it was only a steep hill. Sometimes, we would get stuck in the snow going up the driveway and need to be pulled out with the tractor. Grandmother would be waiting for us at the kitchen doorway. She would have a batch of homemade dough ready to make us fry bread. I could not wait for their first piece, so I put butter and sugar on it. Erich, my brother, and I would eat so much that our stomachs would hurt. We thought Grandmother was the best fry bread maker in the Dakotas. The next day, all of us would go sledding with Grandfather and Tojo the dog. After we were all worn out, we came into the house, and Grandmother would take our wet clothes and mittens and put them near the wood-burning stove in the kitchen. Another adventure would be walking in the woods with Grandfather and Tojo. The best part of the trip was the visit to see the miniature ponies and Lita, the elephant in the historical round red barn.

CHAPTER 3:
CARNIVAL CARAVAN: LATE START

MINN-NO-SO-DAK SHOWS (1970)

I awakened to loud voices outside my window. The voices were getting louder, and one person yelled, *"Get the electrical cords wrapped up and throw them in the truck."* Another voice cried, *"It is already hotter than Mississippi in July."* The sun begins to peek through the homemade pastel, blue-flowered kitchen curtains. I slowly opened my eyes, and my back hurt from cleaning the concession stand last night. I was up until 1:00 am, and now I gazed over at the kitchen clock, which was 7:00 am. Suddenly, my [Aunt Chick], Darlene's nickname, comes barreling into the trailer, "*It's time to move kids, get up and brush your teeth. You only have time to brush your teeth; we're running late.*" I brushed my hair quickly, put it up in a ponytail, put on a t-shirt, and pulled on my worn-out blue jeans. I rolled up my blankets and put the bed under the kitchen table. My Aunt Chick kept the temperature in our Airstream trailer cold due to her asthma. We slept in a sleeping bag with blankets over the top at night. Karman, my sister, wanted to take a shower, but there was no time. The AC would soon be shut off, so you rushed to get out quickly. My Aunt Chick started disconnecting our water hoses and all the electrical cords. We would quickly be on the road to another small town in the Midwest.

Our family carnival, Minn-No-So Dak Carnival, later name changed to Premier Shows, traveled throughout Minnesota, North Dakota, and South Dakota from May to September, bringing carnival food, games, and twenty-two rides for entertainment to these small towns for their small-town fair celebrations. My grandmother was the matriarch of the family. As usual, she was outside in the middle of the carnival grounds, directing everyone with her microphone. She used colorful language to get the job done. She was short in stature with long, beautiful black hair with streaks of gray piled high in a bun. She reviewed the final details with everyone regarding the roads we would travel. Grandmother knew the backroads of the Dakotas like no one else. She grew up on a cattle ranch near Killdeer, ND. Her life was pure poverty, and it entailed work and more work. She broke horses standing up bareback in the creeks.

You could hear Grandmother yelling to everyone, "*We need to get the hell on the road, or we will not make it to the next town before sundown.*" Getting to the town before sundown was essential to connect electricity and water. The mini ponies and the other small animals from the petting zoo needed one final drink of water before loading them into a truck. The lamas, goats, and mini ponies brought smiles to many children. We had names for each pony, but Cookie was my favorite.

We all piled into the old Chevy truck. It had no AC and a difficult stick shift where the fourth gear sometimes slipped, and the radio stations played only country music. My Aunt Chick drove: Jolene, my cousin, sat next to my aunt; my sister Karman was next, and I was next to the window. They usually let me have the window because I spit sunflower seeds out the window and because I was the youngest on the show. I put my feet up on the dashboard and put my sunglasses on, and my aunt handed me a cold Coca-Cola and some leftover popcorn from the stand. I smiled at her and said, "*Thanks, Aunt Chick, a breakfast for champions.*" We rolled the windows down. This was the best part of traveling with my family. We were all musical. My cousin and I would sing "Silver Threads and Golden Needles" and other tunes. I was 13 years old, and it was the summer of 1981. The carnival caravan started down the road. My grandmother was always first in her yellow truck, which I called Beamer. When I rode with her, she let me use the walkie, which was fun. She always wore oversized dark sunglasses and smoked her cigarettes. We followed my grandfather in his old station wagon, pulling his teardrop trailer. You could see his dog, Tojo, sticking his head out the passenger window. Everyone thought he was so poor. However, that was not the case. We had 150 miles to get to the next town.

Sweat started penetrating down the back of my shirt, and the dust from the open fields stuck in my throat. We had water, yet it did not quench my thirst. As we crossed the blue highways in South Dakota and traveled through the Indian Reservations, I saw cars left beside the road and garbage piled high next to trailers—the trailers with broken windows and broken bicycles and trikes. I asked my aunt, "*Why are all these cars along the road? Why do these homes look so sad?*" She said, "*You need to understand what has happened to the Native American people. They were here long before us. Do you want to learn the real history? Listen, and I will tell you?*" My aunt had a degree in history. Along these roads, she told the sad history of the South Dakota Indian tribes.

As we moved through the small towns, people in the streets would stare at us. The trucks hauled the carnival rides, which would take a day to set up. We stopped to fill up with fuel in a small town and all piled out to stretch our legs. My aunt gave me a five-dollar bill and told me to go into the gas station and get us something to drink. Walking into the Standard Station, I noticed older men sitting around a table drinking coffee and wearing Pioneer Seed hats and overalls. The small-town farmers all looked at me and then looked away. I looked for a bathroom and found one in the back of the store. It read, "Out of Order." I went to the glass refrigerator and got four glass-bottled Coca-Colas for us. The woman at the cash register asked me, "*Where are you going with your carnival?*" I said, "*Lemmon, South Dakota.*" She did not smile and appeared haggard and tired due to years of work. I left quickly as I needed to find a bathroom. I asked my aunt, "*The bathroom is out of order; where can I go?*" My aunt said, "*We will find a place soon for you.*" We got back in the truck, and after we were a few miles out of town, my aunt pulled the truck over to the side of the road. She got out and opened my door. "*Here we go; you can head to the cornfield.*" I ran down the ditch through the tall brown grass and reached the cornfield's edge. The corn was taller than me, so I hurried so we could get back on the road. I returned to the truck and asked, "*When will we stop to eat?*" I was getting hungry. Karman and Jolene were five years older than me, and they told me to eat more sunflower seeds. My aunt said, "*In about 30 minutes, we should be there, and then you kids can eat.*"

Along the way, we would sing songs, and my aunt would continue to teach us history and geography. My aunt had a degree in history. She loved to teach us. I could see the town in the distance and knew what I would order from the menu. I thought about how good it would taste and pictured it. I thought about a roast beef sandwich covered with mashed potatoes and a gravy mound. One benefit to eating in these small towns was that they usually had decent food. Only part of the carnival would stop here because there would be too many people if we stopped in one town. Our family would usually stop and eat together. We parked along the small-town streets as people gawked and stared at us. There was a mom-and-pop restaurant down the street. I opened the truck door and could feel the heat on my bare feet. I quickly grabbed my flip-flops. The café window said "open". As we walked inside, the small-town people looked at us as if we were aliens. The booths were old and torn in some places, and the tables had glass rings and coffee stains.

At this point, I was so hungry that I asked my aunt if a hot beef sandwich was on the menu. She was not sure and said we would find out soon. The server came out of the backroom, and her apron looked like it had not been washed for a week. She brought us short Clinton water glasses to our tables. I poured it down my neck. It was cold, but it tasted a little different. A town's water will always taste different. I asked her, "*Do you have a hot beef special?*" She looked at me like I was asking for filet mignon. She responded condescendingly, "*No, we only got what is on the menu. Can you read it?*" My aunt replied, "*Now, you do not need to talk to my baby niece that way. She is at the top of her reading, writing, and arithmetic in her classes. Let's all have a cheeseburger, French fries, and a pitcher of coke.*" It was Coca-Cola or nothing for my aunt. My aunt was like my second mother; she always watched over me and bought me unique things. I spent many of our teenage summer years at the carnival and stayed and worked for her in her concession stand.

We all sat around talking about the next town and the fair board. My grandma said they were a pain to deal with, and she would never play the small town again. My grandma was a straight shooter, and people did not want to be on the wrong side of her. My Uncle Ed, nickname [Bimbo], sat beside my grandmother, wearing his dark sunglasses. He was a forensic psychologist. He told me why he wore dark sunglasses: he could observe people, but people could not see his eyes. He said, "*Kid if people can't see your eyes, they cannot see into your soul. Now, remember that kid.*" I was so hungry but sat patiently waiting for our food. Finally, the server came with our food, and I said, "*Thank you, ma'am.*" She was surprised, and she smiled at me. I devoured my cheeseburger and French fries. Our entire family loves pie, so my aunt called the server over, and she looked annoyed. "*What kind of pie do you have today?*" The server responded, "*We only have one kind left, apple. 2 apple pies back on the counter.*" My aunt replied, "*We will take both pies, please. Give everyone a piece with a big scoop of vanilla ice cream.*" The server said, "*You know that will be an extra cost for the ice cream.*" My aunt said, "*Yes, I do understand. Do you know that your tips are based on your customer service?*" We were treated as uneducated and like we did not know up from down. Little did this person know my family was business-smart and educated. At this young, impressionable age, I discovered that we, as a carnival family, "carnies," were treated with disrespect and second class.

CHAPTER 4:
CARNIVAL CARAVAN: LEMMON, SOUTH DAKOTA

Kristin in Ticket Booth

As we traveled along the South Dakota roads, there were wide open spaces, and some of my favorite songs we would sing were Take Me Home Country Roads, Silver Threads, Golden Needles, and Jolene. My aunt would have me follow the map and tell everyone how many miles from town to town as many signs were not posted. We traveled on US-12 and SD-20 to reach Lemmon, SD, with about one hundred miles left. Getting into town to set up the trucks in the right spots for unloading the rides and trailers to hook up water and electrical cords was essential. I could see the town from a distance, and my aunt told us that Lemmon, SD, is known for the "World's Largest Petrified Wood Park & Museum," and she would make sure we would visit. I was not thrilled about that venture, but my aunt always wanted us to learn about various places.

The carnival caravan slowly moved up the main street, and I peeled my eyes, looking for a laundromat. We had a couple of piles of clothes to wash. This was usually my job. Sometimes, my aunt would buy us new clothes when a town did not have a laundromat. At the end of the summer, I had quite a few clothes to take home. I remember my sister doing the laundry at that laundromat in Lemon. There was no air conditioning in the laundromat. She overloaded a couple of machines and put too much laundry detergent in the machines. The soap spilled onto the floor, and the owner yelled at her, calling her a "stupid carnie kid."

My aunt drove up next to my grandfather because she cared for him first. She connected his electricity to get his AC on and then water hoses. His little dog Tojo was running around his feet, happy to be out of the car. Tojo was trained to do many tricks, and children adored him. We set up our trailer next to Grandfather to watch over him. We moved quickly, knew the routine, and everyone had job tasks. It was an efficient process. By the time we got hooked up, the sun was setting, and we were tired and hungry. We could take showers but were always told to keep them short and not let the hot water run out. I was the last one in the shower that night, and mine was a cold shower, but it still felt good. It was time to eat a bite, and my aunt and I headed for the grocery store for bread, eggs, fruit, strawberry pop tarts, and some boxed theater candy for Karman, Jolene, and me. She always let me pick out a snack I liked. That night, we had egg sandwiches that were the best in Lemmon, South Dakota.

Our water needed to be connected to our concessions trailer the following day. My Aunt Chick asked me to take the gallon bucket and go to the local café. It was not far. I entered the restaurant, and the people sitting at the tables and booths stared at me. They were primarily farmers. I asked the server if I could have a gallon of water for our concession stand. She said, *'So you are from the carnival, right?"* I responded politely, "*Yes, it is my family's carnival.*" She said, "*We don't give water to carnies.*" I was a young kid. I was stunned at her response. I walked out with my empty bucket, and all the eyes in the restaurant followed me. As I walked down the street of Lemmon, South Dakota, I peeked in the windows of the storefronts. It was a typical rural white town.

I got back to the concessions truck. My aunt said, *"Honey, just put the water in the sink."* A small tear started to come down my cheek. I said, "*Aunt Chick, they would not give me water because I am a carnie kid.*" She looked at me. She came over, wiped my tears, and hugged me. "*You follow me back to the café.*" She went into the café with me and our yellow bucket. She approached the server, and now everyone was looking at us. "*I believe you would not give water to my beautiful niece. We come to your town to provide entertainment and a fun place for your children. We come into your town as a family unit. We come into your town, but your minds are closed. You have treated my niece like dirt, and now your café will not get any business from us.*" We had about thirty employees at the time. This invariably means extra business for any small town.

When we returned to the carnival, my grandmother gathered everyone together. Grandmother had a loudspeaker, and when she spoke, people listened. Once everyone gathered around, my aunt said, "*No one will give any business to the café uptown. I will provide the food for the next three days.* " She went to the grocery store and bought items for the meals. This was about 40 people, including our family, but she knew how to cook for a large group. This was the first time I felt like a lower class. I will never forget it as long as I live.

CHAPTER 5:

SCHMIDT FAMILY CIRCUS: GROWING UP UNDER THE BIG TOP

Harold S Schmidt and Rosalita

In the 1950s and 1960s, the Schmidt Family Circus was based in Watertown, South Dakota. From the moment the Circus would come into a small town in South Dakota, Minnesota, or North Dakota, the noise and excitement filled the air. Harold E. Schmidt and Phyliss Maas Schmidt had four children who would become part of the traveling circus.

My father, Harold S. Schmidt, the eldest in the family, started learning to play the accordion at age 5. In his younger years, he would be instrumental in the Circus, playing the instrument for the acts. He was Doodie the Clown at a young age; Doodie translated from German into "Do it." Aunt Darlene was an Acrobat, twirled batons with fire, and a gymnast. My Aunt Boni rode the unicycle and juggled. My Uncle Ed played the saxophone at an early age and juggled. My grandfather did an act with Tojo, the dog, jumping through hoops, rolling on a barrel, and playing the drums.

The tent setup required all kids to help. It required the center poles and outer poles, which were heavy and would be lifted, and the stakes would be pounded in at the bottom. The tent was laced together, and the setup took about an hour and ½ to get done. You could seat three hundred people, and the area at the back of the tent was the menagerie for the wild animals. The stage was at the front with a backdrop.

My father always drove the truck with Rosalita inside the back with an open part at the top section for airflow for Rosalita. The haybale shade was installed beside her. There was a drop tray underneath where her poop would fall into. Farmers would buy elephant poop from my father as it was excellent fertilizer for their soil. My grandfather created all the marketing material to send to small towns to promote the Circus: posters, ride tickets, and announcements in the local papers. I am amazed at what he created because I have these artifacts. He had a vision: to create excitement about the Circus coming to town.

My father asked my grandfather if they could have an elephant for the Circus. My father was about six years of age at that time. When my father was eight years old, a truck pulled into the yard, and my father had just gotten home from school. He could hear a squeal from the back of the truck. He told me. "I thought it was a large pig in there." Then he saw a gray trunk pop out of the truck's back end. My grandpa opened the back of the truck, and there was an actual elephant from Mumbai (Bombay), India. My father was ecstatic and could not believe his eyes that his father bought an elephant for the Circus. It took a long time for her to get through customs and make the trip to Watertown, South Dakota. My grandfather told my father, "You will learn to communicate with her, and it will be like you interact with humankind." My father's best friend would be Rosalita. He sent a letter to the Ringling Brothers Barnum Bailey Circus in Sarasota, Florida. to get specific information on caring for Rosalita. One gentleman would communicate with my father, explaining how to care for Rosalita's skin, feed her the correct hay, and care for her during winter. She lived in the garage, and my father added several hay bales around the garage to keep her warm. Rosalita was so special.

The schoolwork and schoolbooks always came along for their studies, and my grandfather hired a tutor to ensure the kids would learn throughout the summer. They arrived back at the Watertown Public School system a month late. However, my father mentioned, "We were all ahead of the other children because my dad wanted us to work hard and study."

My grandmother encouraged all her children to receive a college education. She encouraged higher education. Each child was exceptional in their field of study. My father received a Master's in German and taught high school German for 46 years at Lincoln High School in Sioux Falls, South Dakota.

Darlene graduated from North Dakota State University with a history degree. Boni graduated from Northern State University, Aberdeen, South Dakota, with an English and teaching degree and taught for several years. Edward graduated with his doctorate in forensic psychology and practiced in the Fergus Falls, MN, area, but he would be involved in several cases throughout Minnesota.

The Circus environment influenced my family members greatly as it was arduous work, and it was through interactions with other people from which they learned a great deal. Each town was different, and the community was different. My father mentioned the towns they played on the Indian Reservations. He said, *"The Indigenous people would come with horses and even buggies in Western North Dakota. It was learning how to interact with other people,"* My grandmother was a woman of strength, and she was the family's matriarch. She instilled in all of us to be kind to all, as you never know where their moccasins have traveled.

CHAPTER 6:
CARNIVAL CARAVAN STORY: OIL SPILL IN CONCESSION STAND

I worked for my Aunt Darlene, and she paid me because I had to buy my items for my school supplies and clothing. My father worked as a German high school teacher in South Dakota, with the country's second lowest teacher salary. My sister worked for my Uncle Ed. She worked on his games and the Spook House. It was long hours, and dealing with the public was sometimes challenging. This is where I truly learned how to work and develop skill sets to help me.

When tearing down our concession stand to prepare to leave, I would ensure the large popcorn oil bottles and the other items used for the concession's food stand were secured with tarp straps. We pulled the concession stand behind our truck. We also had the Airstream to drive, which many times was an employee.

As we left for Fairmount, North Dakota, we were in route to Flaxton, North Dakota, for the Burke County Fair. I know I was in a hurry that morning to finish all my duties because my aunt told us to hurry up as we were behind schedule. When we entered Flaxton and found our location for setup, I jumped out and knew exactly what I needed to do. It was always the electrical cords first for power, followed by the heavy water hoses for the water. After I completed this, I opened the door to the concession stand. The door to the popcorn oil was open. I had failed to tarp them and secure the cap on one large container. Popcorn oil was all over the floor. It was about a ½ inch thick. I almost fell onto the floor. I immediately thought, "Oh boy, this is not good because we needed to prepare for opening that night." I grabbed a bucket and turned on the boxed fan in the back of the stand. I got towels to start wiping it up. I was drenched in popcorn oil.

I heard my aunt calling my name. I was a little worried as to what she would say. She looked in the concessions stand. She started to laugh. She said, "*Baby, it looks like you had a bath with popcorn oil.*" I said, "*Aunt Chick, I am so worried you would be mad at me. I did not secure the oil, and one bottle was open.*" She said, "*Are you hurt?*" I responded, "*No.*" She said, *"That is all I care about, Kris. If you are okay, that is all that matters. This is nothing, and you are trying to clean it up. I love you. You will also learn to ensure that the containers are secure and the lids are tight.*" I stood there with a tear as if I had the best aunt in the world. It took me 2 hours to clean it up, and my aunt found a product to help absorb the oil. I headed to the shower, the longest shower of my entire life. My hair was still greasy, even after shampooing it several times. It was an excellent moisturizer.

Once we were ready for customers that evening, I could smell the buttered popcorn as people lined up for carnival food. The caramel apples were displayed in a 3-level tray. Some had nuts, and some were just made of delicious caramel. The cotton candy was hung on a string on one side for all to see. Pink, yellow, and blue cotton candy colors were on a white stick. Karman, my sister, made the cotton candy earlier in the day. One time, she accidentally dropped a quarter in the machine, and it broke. It was shut down. My Uncle Bill drove to Fargo, North Dakota, to get the part. It was about two hundred miles one way from the town. My uncle never got upset with us; he loved us. My uncle brought all the supplies from Fargo to our location. He was efficient and knew the inventory.

He needed to bring us sugar, caramel, hotdogs, apples, popcorn, syrup for soda, and other items.

My aunt would have me try to "market" our food by walking down the midway with popcorn and a caramel apple. She said she wanted people to see our food and for me to talk to the people about where the concession stand was. People wonder why I am an extrovert. My aunt always stressed the need to keep our counters clean. She was very particular about food preparation and keeping the stand clean. I learned so many valuable lessons from my aunt and uncle. Be kind to all customers, even if they are not kind to you. Treat everyone the same. I learned to work hard. Most of all, I have many fond memories of life traveling on a carnival with my family. There were moments of laughter, challenges, scary inclement weather, and tears, but we loved one another.

Darlene

Because of the schedule, we would be called thirty milers, and the caravan would only drive thirty miles daily. Some towns had only 250 people, and some had 2,000 people. Some of the towns wanted us, and some did not. We left in mid-May and returned to Watertown, SD, in mid-September. Our home was the Circus, and our playground was the Circus. We did all the performing; there were no outside performers. It was a family Circus.

My brother, Harold's nickname [Butch], and I would climb to the top of the tent, slide down, grab a lacing just before the edge, and stop. Do you know how dangerous that was? The tent was a trampoline for us. Butch and I would play on top of the tent when our parents went to town for supplies. Climbing was challenging, as the side poles were six feet tall. We would sit on top of the tent, look at the skyline, and tell stories to one another. If the tent were loose, we could use it as a trampoline. We did not know its dangers.

Later, we would take a quarter and run to the grocery store to get a loaf of bread. We would drop pieces around Rosalita and jump on top of her. She would get sick of me and Butch and push us off. We would grab her leg and move with her. She was a kind and gentle animal. Her trunk, with a little nipple on the end of it, touched our faces.

We did not have friends. Our friends were our animals. We used to make it into a playground. We took an old board and made a teeter-totter. Never went to the parks. People always asked us personal questions, whether we had a house, went to school, or knew how to read—all the questions we wanted to avoid answering the people. We just wanted to stay in the Circus lot. The family was a unit of cohesiveness, love, and talent. The labor was unforgiving. People would bring their kids down and watch us work. This work was never-ending. It was hard labor, and we never thought of it as it was all we knew. This was our livelihood. It was a hard life. We were born into this. The talent was in our DNA.

Every evening, my dad used to sit with his black notebook. I had to do so many backbends and acrobats. He wrote it down. I would say, "Did you get it down in the book?" He would sit there day in and day out with all of us: Boni-juggling and unicycle. We had to be disciplined. When it was time for us to perform, we had to drop everything when we heard the generator start, as the show was starting soon. The generator went off at the show's end and was completely dark. We looked up at the stars, walked to our trucks, and would fall fast asleep from the long days.

CHAPTER 8:

SCHMIDT FAMILY CIRCUS: POW WOW- DARLENE TELLS THE STORY.

I climbed out of my sleeper. My dad had built this little sleeper in the truck box above the truck, but I overtook it and put a mattress in it. A small window, a small nail to shut and close it, to climb out of it. I would put my foot on the truck handle—a Mason jar of water for my teeth. I named my truck Betsy. All our trucks had names. The roads we traveled were gravel and blue highways. I started driving at the age of thirteen. The truck had a rusty floorboard; the dust would come up, and the heat would come up through the floorboard. It felt like hell on earth, if that is what it is like. I climbed out my window. I noticed my mother and her cousin Floyd Maas talking quite a bit, more than usual.

My dad loaded up Rosalita, and I got into my truck. What were they talking about? The town we were in was isolated. It was small. A café and a tiny bank were about it; we had a caravan as I drove out of town. My mother was first, and her trailer and her car, myself driving Betsy, Butch with Rosalita, Floyd, Uncle Mike, and Dad was last. As I went out of town, I noticed there were fewer and fewer telephone poles. I used to count them for something to do. But as we drove on, I saw no grain or corn fields. I kept thinking about where we were going.

There was nothing around. I followed my mother's taillights, and soon, she put the brake on. The telephone poles had ceased. I noticed the grass was dry and begging for a drink of water. No trees, no birds, I was worried. We went only 20 miles per hour. The sun was beating down on all of us. As we drove up, the shack read, "Trading Post USA." A knife scratched out the USA portion. The shack had no paint on it, and it looked completely dead. It looked like a place of pain and suffering. Mom pulled up, and a tall man with long black hair emerged. I could hear a generator start up in the back of the shack. I knew there was no electricity in this remote location. We were on an Indian Reservation, and the tribe would have a big pow-wow. I had just seen Pow Wow in a movie, but I thought they were just in the film, not a real thing that took place. I asked my mom, *"There are no people here for the Pow Wow."*

Mom responded, *"You just wait and see."* I asked the tall man if they had water, and he pointed to where to go. I walked about one hundred feet out and saw a pit. There were some steps made of rock built in. I walked down the steps to a faucet. I washed myself off and took a drink. You can get sick on the water. I returned and knew work was beginning to put the tent up. We had sections of the tent to lace together. Boni, my sister, and I would do the lacings. There was a piece of rope, and you could not miss one eyelet; otherwise, this would leave a section of the tent unsecured. The sun was so hot, and I could feel the sun beating down on us. I was lacing and lacing. I looked up, and there was this vast dust in the distance. They came on horses, pickups, and old cars. This was in the mid-1950s.

Then, in the distance, I saw dust coming up and several vehicles, horses, and trucks. All the Native Americans circled us. All at once, all the people stopped before they got to the building. Here came this old pickup; driving fast, we were told he was the tribe chief. He got out and started pointing here and there—pickups of wood, hay, water. I could not believe my eyes. They started putting up their teepees. They said that our teepee was a giant—teepee. I laughed. My dad was worried; Rosalita had no grass; he talked to the trader. They brought some hay for her. My dad rubbed the hay together and tasted a bit of hay. He said the hay was good for Rosalita to eat; she could get sick if it had something that would not tolerate her system.

In the daytime, the women danced. I learned to dance with them. They called me a toe head because of my blonde hair. We loved dancing with them. The people were so kind, gentle, and happy. They had a scarcity of everything but were happy to celebrate a pow-wow piece of their culture together. It was the lousy land that they were forced to live on.

After the show that night, the men danced. The dresses were made of genuine leather and were colorful, and the people were so proud of their culture. The children danced and laughed. Then, the long, narrow bonfire was lit up. They were cooking. The food was prepared. My mom would not let us eat it because she did not want us to get sick, so we could not perform. It was late, and my dad said I had to go to bed. I crawled up into my little sleeper and looked out my window. It is so beautiful to watch the flickering bonfire. I looked up at the sky and saw the upside-down candles, which I called the stars. This was our only light on the Circus. The following day, I climbed down, and everyone was getting ready to leave. The land was so barren, but the people were so good and honorable.

CHAPTER 9:
REFLECTIONS ON THE THREAD OF THE CIRCUS IN ALL OF US

Our family entertained many generations throughout the Midwest, starting in the 1930s with my grandfather and his One-Man Band. My father, two aunts, and uncle became part of the Schmidt Family Circus based in Watertown, South Dakota. The family entertained in the 1950s and 1960s, moving from town to town to bring a menagerie of animal performances. They brought laughter to the people of the Midwest. In the mid-1960s, it was converted into a carnival caravan based in Dalton, Minnesota. It grew over the years into a mid-size carnival with twenty-one rides, games, and two concession stands. Our bedtime stories from my father would be stories of him growing up under the big top. He talked about when Tommy the Lion clawed his neck, or Rosalita got sick from children feeding her junk food. Rosalita was the part of the show that everyone adored. Those stories are near and dear to my heart. Yes, our family worked long hours and led a unique life, but our family loved animals like humans. Our family is talented in music and other areas that are in our DNA from my grandfather. I see it in the great-grandchildren. My daughter, Marianna Schmidt, was the fourth generation to work on the carnival. She said, "*Mom, it was the hardest work. I worked for Uncle Ed on the duck pond and the children's rides. There were times when I just wanted to come home.*" She learned how to work and appreciated a hot shower. I was always ashamed to tell people I grew up on a traveling carnival. I am not ashamed to share the stories and the love that we had as a family.

The Circus will live on in all of us.

Kristin and Grandma

Life is Like a River

As you move along the river, there are rocks you will need to avoid.

As you move along the river, there might be a current you need to endure.

You may need to adjust your direction as the river bends and moves.

As you move through it, you will encounter a storm, fog, or a burst of beautiful sunshine.

Experience life like the river, and let the river be your guide.

Written by Kristin Schmidt Larson

My grandmother inspired this poem. In one of my last conversations with her before she passed away. She spoke to me about the river and how it would help me. I think of her now during these times and hear her say, "Remember the currents that you will need to endure."